TAI-OTOSHI

Cross-grip *tai-otoshi*—my specialty. 1983 British Open.

JUDO MASTERCLASS TECHNIQUES

Tai-Otoshi

Neil Adams

with
Eddie Ferrie

Photographs by David Finch

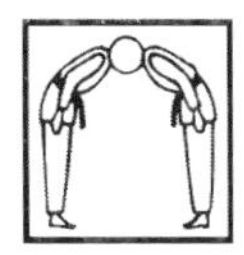

Ippon Books

First published by
Ippon Books Ltd.
HR House
447 High Road
North Finchley
London N12 0AF

British Library in Cataloguing in Publication Data

Adams, Neil
Tai-Otoshi: Judo Masterclass Techniques
1. Judo
2. Title

ISBN 1-874572-21-6

ACKNOWLEDGEMENTS:

Many thanks to Eddie Ferrie who helped me write this book. His writing skills and judo experience make him an invaluable member of the Ippon Books team.

And my thanks to my students at the Neil Adams Judo Club who served as my ukes for the photo session.

Managing Editor: Nicolas Soames
Production Editor: Oon Yeoh
Design & Layout: Graham Rawlings
Photographer: David Finch
Printer: Redwood Books, Towbridge

Contents

Peter Seisenbacher won the first of his two Olympic gold medals with this splendidly timed *tai-otoshi* against Robert Berland of the USA. 1984 Los Angeles Olympics.

FOREWORD

Tai-Otoshi is one of the great classical judo throws. There, along with *seoi-nage*, *osoto-gari* and *uchimata* is *tai-otoshi*. One reason is that it is a throw that can be done—and is done—by all weight categories. It is a throw that a small person can do by utilizing his speed to whip over an opponent; it is a throw that a large person can do by utilizing his upper body control and drawing a lighter opponent over.

Few world champions can be said to have such a mastery of the technique as Britain's 1981 world light middleweight champion, Neil Adams. He threw most of his opponents at one time or another with *tai-otoshi*, either as a direct attack, or in combination with one of his other major throws, such as *uchimata* or *kouchi-gari*. And it was significant that his very last throw in competition—in the 1988 Olympics in Seoul—was *tai-otoshi*. He scored *ippon*.

Adams studied the technique ever since, as a teenager, his father ordered him to switch from *morote-seoi-nage* which was damaging his back. This decision to change was one of the great stepping-stones on the way to a top competition career which encompassed two Olympic silver medals and six European titles.

Adams is regarded, even now, as one of the great stylists of our time. Yet, interestingly, he points out that his way of executing *tai-otoshi* is not totally classical. He made a virtue of the wide, flat stance, combining, in a totally balanced way, speed into the technique, hand control and finishing power. Certainly, no one who has experienced his *tai-otoshi* will ever forget the sense of inevitability in that flash of a moment before the technique actually connected.

It is perhaps because of this that Adams is the ideal person to detail the rich field of *tai-otoshi*, from the most traditional to the latest in attacking moves and attacking grips. Fifteen years at the very top of the competition ladder, and now growing experience as a leading international coach, can only result in the definitive book on the subject.

Nicolas Soames
Masterclass Series Editor

A Personal View

Tai-otoshi is a particularly difficult technique to master, yet for me it is the quintessence of what good judo is all about. It is an *ippon* scoring technique, a dynamic, big, bold throwing movement that requires you to turn your back on your opponent. It requires speed, co-ordination and timing as well as an element of risk. *Tai-otoshi* is classed as a *tewaza*, a hand technique yet the whole body has to co-ordinate as a smooth and efficient unit; the hips should be supple and there should be spring in the legs. It is a throw well worthy of study, requiring many thousands of repetitions both in *uchikomi* and *nage-komi* to perfect it. Once mastered though, it is difficult to predict, let alone block and there have been many examples of fighters pulling an unexpected *tai-otoshi* out of the hat, to completely change the course of a match.

a) David Starbrook: *tai-otoshi* specialist.

When I was a youngster my favourite technique was *morote-seoi-nage*, but as I grew taller I began to pick up too many little injuries and I started to have problems with increasing pains in my back at about the stage when I got my brown belt. Luckily my father always kept a close eye on what I was getting up to, and he suggested that I should switch to *tai-otoshi* instead. He was right too, because splitting my legs meant that the pressure in my back was released and my back problems disappeared.

b) Starbrook and his famous "wrong leg" *tai-otoshi*.

It took a lot of persistence to make the *tai-otoshi* work, especially in contest and it was at least a year before I was confident of using it in serious contests. When I was a junior international I used to see top fighters scoring *ippon* with it time and again. My predecessor in the British team, Dave Starbrook, had an excellent *tai-otoshi* which he used to great effect at the 1976 Montreal Olympics. He was famous for being able to complete the technique even if his opponent managed to step over his blocking leg. Starbrook's success with *tai-otoshi* helped to confirm my belief that it was an important weapon to have in my arsenal.

Tai-otoshi is a technique that required a lot of practice to get right, with a lot of attention to detail, particularly almost intangible factors like feeling and timing, but when it worked it scored spectacularly. In 1977 I threw the strong Russian Tamaz Namgalauri for *ippon* with *tai-otoshi* in the German Junior Open, which confirmed it as an

Coming to grips with Vladimir Nevzerov, an expert at *tai-otoshi*. Notice the cross-grip—Nevzerov prefers to attack from this grip, something I later adopted as well.

effective technique for me. In the same year I fought a draw with Vladimir Nevzerov, the reigning senior world champion—and a *tai-otoshi* expert—who I was really hungry to beat. I actually knocked him down with *tai-otoshi* and the referee awarded a *koka*, but the line judges overruled him and it was waived. I fought him again the next day and he attacked me like a man possessed, taking a fairly convincing win and I never got another chance to beat him, as he retired not long after, but the *tai-otoshi* was the throw that had taken me closest to beating him.

The first major senior competition where it worked for me was the 1978 European Championships. At the time I was still only a junior, albeit the European junior champion. I remember fighting the East German, Gunther Kruger in the semi-final and threw him for a *yuko* with drop *seoi-nage*. Unfortunately I was soon given a *chui* for passivity—unfairly I felt—and he was awarded the contest. Feeling that I had been robbed of a place in the final I went out to fight in the repechage with something to prove. My opponent for the bronze medal was the brilliant Russian fighter Valeri Dvoinikov, but I was really fired up and out to prove something. I gave him absolutely no respect. Soon after the start I threw him for a *yuko* with *tai-otoshi*. When he stood up, almost immediately, I banged him over for *ippon* with another *tai-otoshi*. I remember the expression of disbelief on the face of British Team Coach Tony Macconnell as I came of the mat, but there were many more *ippons* to come from *tai-otoshi*.

Takahiro Nishida, the superb Japanese lightweight.

As you practise and compete year in and year out your techniques come and go to a certain extent. As your opponents study your style and try to frustrate your best techniques you constantly have to come up with something extra or new to keep on winning. *Tai-otoshi* worked for me year in and year out. Often too I was able to score *ippon* with other techniques because my opponents had to concentrate so much on avoiding *tai-otoshi.* In the 1978 Kano Cup I fought the brilliant Japanese Takahiro Nishida who, although never a world or Olympic champion, was, in my opinion, the best - 71 kg fighter in the world at the time. He was certainly my most dangerous opponent. His gripping was excellent and he was one of the very few men I have fought who was able to knock me down at will in *randori.* Perhaps he was a little overconfident, fighting in front of his home crowd or perhaps it was a case of my feeling I had nothing to lose, but from the referee's call of *hajime* I went straight out and attacked him. I made two really fast, hard *tai-otoshi* attacks and he just stepped over them, almost nonchalantly. The next attack I made must have felt like another *tai-otoshi* because he went to step the same way and I threw him for *ippon* with one of the best *uchimatas* I have ever done, much to the shock and disappointment of the Japanese crowd. Everyone remembers the *uchimata,* but I was only able to do it because he had perceived the *tai-otoshi* as the real threat!

Waldemar Legien, double Olympic champion.

In 1985 in the semi-final of the German Open I fought the skilful Polish champion Waldemar Legien, who would go on to become a double Olympic gold medalist and threw him for *ippon* with *tai-otoshi* in seven seconds flat! He did not even have time to take a hold and was really annoyed with himself afterwards, but that kind of precise, unpredictable technique is almost impossible to defend against.

Perhaps nowadays there is a little too much emphasis placed on physical preparation and conditioning and with everyone rushing to get physically stronger not enough energy is devoted to developing rhythm, balance, timing, proper positioning and the use of the opponent's reactions. These more intangible aspects of a skill tend to be easily forgotten if they are not highlighted by the coach in technique training sessions.

Correctly done *tai-otoshi* should have the sudden incisive quality typical of a good footsweep. There is minimum body contact and the opponent should not feel the actual technique until it is too late and his back is hitting the mat. Badly executed *tai-otoshi* sometimes turn into *makikomi* actions or break down into attempts to drag the opponent to the floor, but such attacks are anti-judo, in my opinion. A good *tai-otoshi* is characterised by speed, timing, skill, style and flair.

a) A perfect entry to *tai-otoshi*.

b) Although my opponent manages to fall on his right knee…

c) …I am able to complete the rotation with my arms..

1985 Hamar European Championships.

There are numerous reasons why *tai-otoshi* is such a difficult throw for many people to do, the most obvious being that it is generally very badly taught. In trying to develop a good *tai-otoshi* it is vital to aim for perfection, while remaining prepared to compensate for imperfections as we come across them.

One of the main reasons for doing this book was to pool together some of the main teaching points that can make the difference between success and failure at whatever level—whether it be a club practice or an international contest. I also feel it is important to make a permanent record of some of the technical developments which have taken place since Trevor Leggett and Kisaburo Watanabe wrote their truly excellent book "Championship Judo—Tai-Otoshi and O-Uchi-Gari Attacks" over 30 years ago. As a study in how to develop general attacking movement I don't think it has ever been equalled. However this book aims to develop further the work done in that volume and to look at how the world's top competitors over the last 30 years have used and developed the classical *tai-otoshi* to suit their own styles and physiques under the pressure of competition in, at times, quite surprising ways.

A good teacher should put across good teaching points and one of the first things judo players should be told about *tai-otoshi* is that it is a very positive attacking movement which is very difficult to counter. Attention to detail is something that I feel is so important in judo. Many players put in enormous amounts of effort into their training, but often it is misdirected. It is relatively easy to go and do an hour's weight training or go for a five mile run, because they are comparatively mindless activities. To do an hour's intelligent skill training is much more difficult. The real difficulty in fact is that you cannot teach yourself judo, which is where the coach, teacher or *sensei* comes in.

Even top competitors frequently have serious technical deficiencies and quite often are not even aware of what they are. It is very easy to say to young judo players that they should aim for technical perfection, but they need to have a very clear idea, a model of what technical perfection entails. Sometimes they misguidedly base their efforts on what they have seen work in competition, little realising that sometimes techniques which are seriously flawed can be made to come off by a gifted athlete or someone with freakish genetic advantages.

With *tai-otoshi* I would like to try and re-establish a technical standard. This book is the product of a combination of techniques, ideas, methods, approaches and judo knowledge accumulated over 30 years of training, competing and coaching at the highest levels and I hope it contains something of interest to everyone who practises judo.

An early variation of *tai-otoshi*. Notice that the stance is not very wide at all.

History of Tai-otoshi

Tai-otoshi is one of the fundamental throwing techniques in judo. It was originally taught as the fifth technique of the first *kyo* in the original *go-kyo* of 1895. When the *go-kyo* was modified in 1920 it was moved to the second *kyo* and since then has been taught as the sixth technique in that group.

Tai-otoshi is classed as a *tewaza* or hand technique because the essence of an effective *tai-otoshi* is in the throwing action as directed by the hands. In fact in Jigoro Kano's *Kodokan Judo*, it is demonstrated in the photographic sequence without any leg contact between *tori* and *uke* whatsoever. An additional, later photograph has been added showing what is now regarded as the classical *tai-otoshi* position with *tori*'s leg in front of *uke*, forming an obstacle for him to be thrown over by the hands, but this is quite absent in the original demonstration.

Kyuzo Mifune performing *tai-otoshi* without leg contact.

It is very interesting to compare this early demonstration of *tai-otoshi* with both *uki-otoshi* and *sumi-otoshi* as there are subtle but definite links between these three throws as they were originally conceived. When pondering the inclusion of *tai-otoshi* among *tewaza* it is as well to bear in mind that in many strong *tai-otoshi* attacks, even when the defender manages to step over the thrower's outstretched leg, he still gets thrown by the turning action of the hands.

Techniques come in and out of fashion in judo, for many reasons. Hikoichi Aida 8th dan in his *Method of Kodokan Judo* which was translated by E.J. Harrison over 35 years ago refers to 'the current vogue for *tai-otoshi*'! Certainly it belongs among the major throws in the judo tradition in Great Britain.

Photographs of early *tai-otoshi* examples from the era of the ju-jitsu challenges in the music halls often indicate that the technique as it originally appeared was higher and required less athleticism or flexibility than is now the case, probably because people then were inclined to stand more upright making them easier to throw with this technique. Also the early ju-jitsu men were very short and probably did not need to get very low in order to get under their usually much taller opponents.

In Meiji times *tai-otoshi* was taught with the leg almost straight and the weight supported on the inside edge of the foot. This fell out of favour because the knee was placed in a vulnerable position and in competitions in Japan there were some injuries as a result.

A ju-jitsu photograph of a technique resembling *tai-otoshi*. Notice the very straight blocking leg as *tori* draws *uke* over.

Currently *tai-otoshi* is taught with the emphasis on being mechanically safe and avoiding the danger of any knee injuries. Done in this way, with the throwing leg bent at the knee and the weight on the ball of the foot and toes, the hip is angled in such a way that should a defender collapse, or drop on your leg in desperation to avoid being thrown the knee will simply bend and the likelihood of a knee injury is slight. This, incidentally was the way, Kisaburo Watanabe did his *tai-otoshi*, except in a more extreme form. He used to get right underneath his opponents, bending the legs so that the knee of the attacking leg almost touched the floor. He would use his entire bodyweight dropping at speed to draw his opponents completely off balance, then his legs would spring straight to spin them over onto their backs, controlling their fall all the way to the ground with a very positive, aggressive hand action.

Kisaburo Watanabe and his bent leg *tai-otoshi*. From this position he would spring up to complete the throw.

Yasuhiro Kai (JPN) attacks with full commitment. Notice how he is leaning completely forward as he executes the technique. Such commitment is necessary to make *tai-otoshi* work.

The Basics

When techniques are being studied it is good to adopt a whole-part-whole approach in both teaching and practice. The experienced teacher usually demonstrates the whole technique in a movement situation then picks out certain key elements which he emphasizes, such as the grip, action of the head, turn of the hips and so on and encourages individual students to pay attention to those areas where their technique needs to be improved. Having studied important points like grip, feet positions, directions of pull, footwork, movement patterns it is a good idea to aim to develop a general feeling for the technique before getting too bogged down in minor technical details. When doing *uchikomi* though it is always good to concentrate on what you are trying to achieve rather than just crashing in any old how. Each repetition should aim to be a perfect movement, identical to the one before and the one that comes after. Repetition alone does not produce good technique, in fact bad repetitions will result in a faulty technique. Good technique comes from good repetitions, so always aim for quality.

Correct grip and posture combined with good movement is part of the key to developing an effective *tai-otoshi*. This can be developed by doing lots of *uchikomi*, in the early stages with a static partner and later on, increasingly, on the move. Static *uchikomi* is good in the early stages to teach correct leg movements and hip positioning, but more realistic movement situations ought to be introduced as soon as possible. Even the addition of moving *uchikomi* is not enough and all such training must be complemented by *nage-komi*, (repetition throwing) so that trainees actually get to perform the complete movement. Obviously a sprung floor is especially desirable for this kind of training. Unfortunately they are the exception rather than the rule in many dojos and while the crash mat can be used to good effect to practise many other throws, unfortunately it does not lend itself to the effective practise of repetition throwing where *tai-otoshi* is concerned.

Like any technique the throwing action in *tai-otoshi* can usually be broken down into its component parts, but in the first instance the relative stances of *tori* and *uke* have to be looked at. What *tori* does when he attacks is very much determined by the way *uke* grips and stands. The Japanese identify two basic situations *ai-yotsu* and *kenka-yotsu*. *Ai-yotsu* is translated as same grips, and describes two cases i) where both players grip right-handed ii) where both players are left handed. *Kenka-yotsu* (different grips) describes the situation where one player grips left handed and the other right handed. Many judo players in the west often stand more or less square on to their opponents and the only indication as to whether they are right or left handed is the placement of the hands when they grip. Japanese players tend to favour a posture where one side of the body is forward, effectively standing sideways on to their opponent. It is very important to be clear about the grips and stances in these examples of *tai-otoshi* as a change of stance or grip can make a given version of the throw unworkable, but open the door to another of its variations. As an illustration, right *tai-otoshi* was always one of my favourite techniques against right-handed fighters, but it was usually extremely difficult for me to do it against extreme left handers such as Ezio Gamba of Italy or Nobutoshi Hikage of Japan. Part of the challenge of judo is to come up with answers to difficult, frustrating situations, awkward grips—and arms like iron bars that seem only to aim to hold you off are all part of the game.

Grips

One of the keys to effective throwing technique is an effective grip. The basic sleeve/lapel grip is generally the preferred one for *tai-otoshi*, but it is often necessary to fight to get that grip.

Breaking Uke's Lapel Grip

Some fighters when aware of the danger of being thrown by a big forward technique will try to avoid the problem by taking a lapel grip with the left hand then keeping the right sleeve back out of reach. This type of player often makes repeated, not particularly effective attacks with drop *seoi-nage* and makes for a very boring practice.

By simply gripping my own right lapel with my left hand and twisting to my left I can break his grip on my lapel.

By then raising my right elbow I can pull myself in and get close enough to reach for his right sleeve without any danger of him attacking effectively because he has not got a grip. This often makes him feel very insecure because his mind is occupied with how to get a hold with his left hand again, which is what makes him comfortable, being his favoured, safe grip. This simple tactic also often provokes *uke* to try to grip with his right hand. Once he tries this he places his sleeve in a position where I can take my grip.

The Slip I

This is a useful method for nullifying a potentially dangerous lapel grip. *Uke* takes my left lapel in his right hand, a grip which will allow him to mount an effective attack if he also gets his sleeve grip.

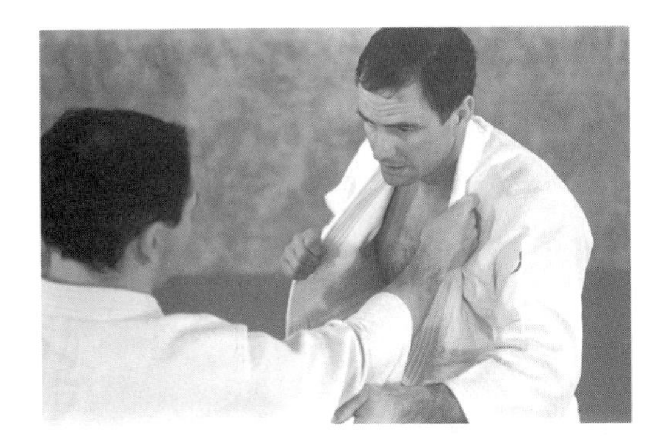

To reduce his effectiveness I take my right lapel in my right hand, pulling it free of the belt and slip it around my shoulders, so that his hand instead of controlling my lapel at the upper chest, which is an attacking grip, slips down to just above waist level which is essentially a defensive position.

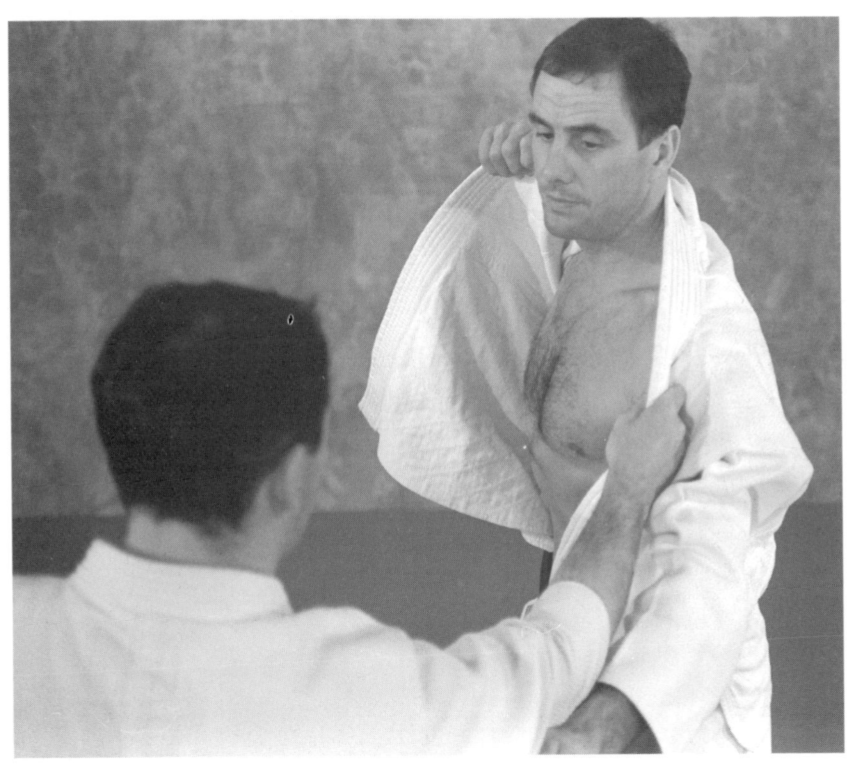

Now I can impose my own right hand grip on him.

The Slip II

This is a surprisingly effective technique which is very frustrating for my opponent.

a) Often *uke* will try to inch his way up my left lapel if I have only allowed him to grip low down.

b) Unfortunately for him each time he inches his hand higher up the lapel he has to release his grip to do so. In that split second when he relaxes his grip, I grip his right wrist with my right hand.

c) I can now use both my hands to snap off his high grip and thrust it down low again, regaining the initiative.

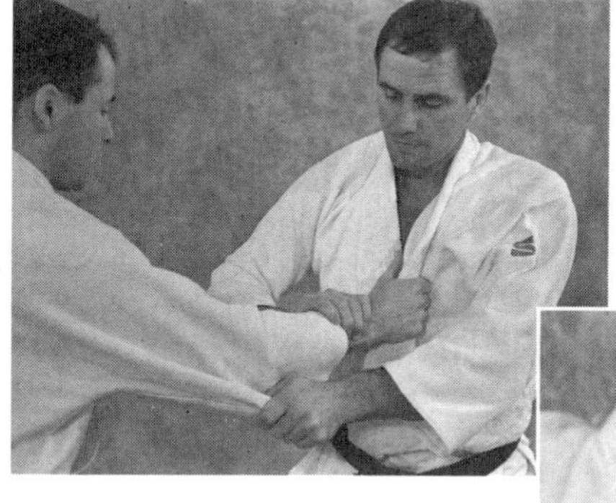

d) Now, I can impose my own grips on him.

Against Upper Grip

a) The action of the *tsurite* is crucial in opening up his defence and it will be determined by who has the upper grip. Here my opponent has the upper grip.

b) If *uke* has the upper grip my right arm must make a shrugging movement to make his arm move out to the side, freeing my right shoulder and so allowing me to begin to turn.

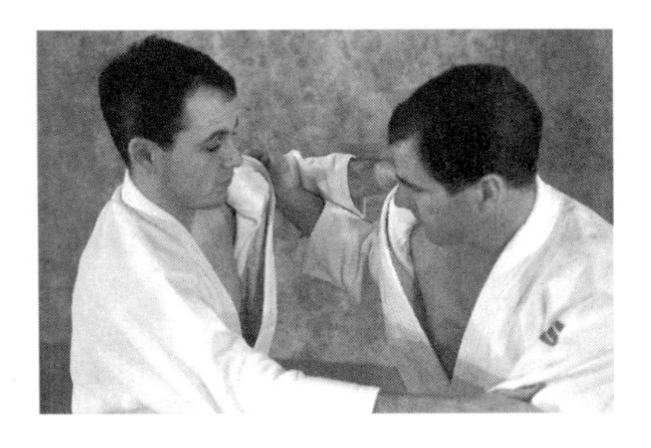

c) As I turn his left arm no longer controls my upper body and bends at the elbow as I come in.

Against Under Grip

a) If *uke* takes the under grip and prefers to hold my right lapel lower down the problem is different and a different solution is called for.

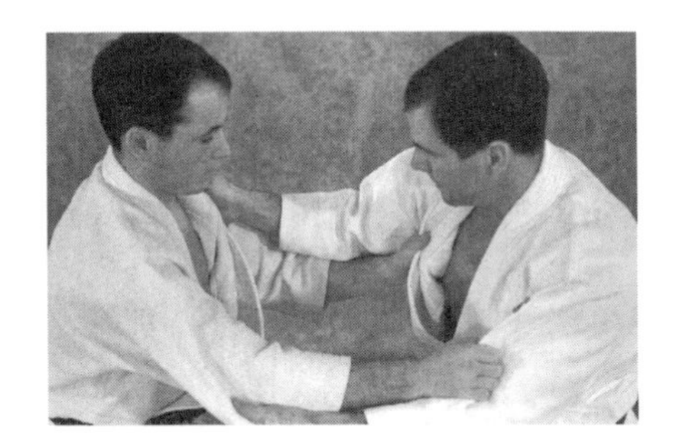

b) I simply slip my right elbow over the crook of his arm and push it down and out. If he does not release his grip his arm is trapped as I turn in for the throw making escape very difficult.

c) If he releases he gives me the opportunity to make an unobstructed attack. Once you choose to employ this kind of gripping gambit it is very important to press your advantage home and actually make the attack, otherwise you will have wasted a good chance.

Head Position

One of the fundamental mistakes many people make when practising *tai-otoshi* is that they lose their balance.The reason why this happens can usually be attributed either to incorrect positioning of the head or positioning of the feet.

The biggest mistake in the use of the head is that of turning it and looking over the left shoulder. There are times when the head goes in this direction in order to bring off a throw, but it is normally as an adjustment to an opponent's defence. This same incorrect positioning of the head is often coupled with a tendency to throw the left foot back to such an extent that it is both outside and parallel with *uke*'s left foot. This usually means that *tori* occupies the same line as *uke*, so while it may look like a good, committed deep attack there is no real positional advantage. When you throw with *tai-otoshi* the head should be directly between the base formed by your feet and it should travel in the direction you want to throw *uke*.

The Legs

On one of my training stays in Japan I was at the Kodokan at the same time as Robert van de Walle and we were both invited to demonstrate how we did our favourite techniques. Shozo Fujii, one of the Japanese team coaches and four times world champion, asked me to demonstrate *tai-otoshi*. I understood why he was curious to see my way of doing it. I had a similar situation when the South Korean national team came to The Budokwai, the famous London club, to practise and the coach asked exactly the same kind of questions. I have noticed that in Japan and in Asia, in general, *tai-otoshi* is usually taught in a different way to that which is popular in Europe. Generally when the turn is made Japanese and South Korean fighters tend to leave a gap and the opponent is pulled forwards off balance—he is tripped by the leg which essentially has a blocking function. The hips do not open laterally, but turn and open front to back as when doing a lunge; the toes of the right leg are usually turned in and the knee bends in such a way that if the opponent were to defend by dropping on the leg, it would simply bend the way it is designed to, minimising the risk of injury.

The traditional way

a) There is a small gap between my blocking leg and *uke*'s right leg.

b) I have pulled forwards—he will trip over my blocking leg.

Neil Adams's way
My way of doing *tai-otoshi* has always been quite different and the right leg has a much more important role in bringing off the technique.

a) I always aim to strike my opponent's shin, just below the knee with the back of my calf/knee, trapping his leg.

b) I then bend slightly more, getting right underneath him and as I pull with the arms, drive the leg straight, and jack my opponent up on his toes.

c) This lifting action springs his foot clear off the mat so that he can neither step nor block.

Tip: Other judo teachers often query the relatively higher risk of a knee injury from attacking this way, but I always stress the importance of the speed of the technique and strength of the braced leg. It is very important that the toes do not point inwards to allow the hips to open easily and quickly and I also stress the importance of practising the leg contact in *uchikomi*. I remember watching Dave Starbrook doing his *uchikomi* against the post in the Renshuden Judo Club, and I was convinced of the effectiveness of the lifting leg *tai-otoshi* although obviously the legs need to be thoroughly conditioned.

The Arms

Perhaps the most important part of a good *tai-otoshi* is the use of the hands to turn the opponent. Not everyone finds the hand action simple and straightforward. A good drill, especially for children and beginners, is to teach the hand action as part of a groundwork technique. It is doubly useful for building confidence because it teaches people to finish the technique without involving a heavy fall for *uke*.

Arm Drill

a) Starting from the kneeling position I take my basic sleeve/lapel grip.

b) I extend my right leg to the side and give a little push to *uke*'s left to get a reaction.

c) I then pull hard and twist my body to my left, pulling *uke* off-balance as I drive with my right leg.

d) *Uke* is pulled over to his right side.

VARIATIONS

This chapter deals with some of the different versions of *tai-otoshi* that have proven to be effective over the years. One of the great things about judo is the sheer variety of technique that results from individual players with different body types and physical characteristics adapting the basic forms to suit their particular needs and strengths. There is no one, exclusive, correct way to do *tai-otoshi*, simply because people and the situations they find themselves in combat are different. But having said that it is important to identify the form that best suits you and your particular physical characteristics and allows you to achieve the best results. Teachers, who in their pasts have been champions, often do not teach what they actually did in competition themselves, frequently because long experience has shown them, that the majority of their students will be unable to duplicate the techniques that they themselves found so appropriate and easy. The important thing then is that the teacher should create the conditions in which the student can generate his own *ippon* scoring technique. This is best achieved by attention to basics and by employing training methods that will help to develop rhythm and timing as well as just technique.

Trailing Tai-Otoshi

This is the basic, direct form of *tai-otoshi* I used against opponents who gripped right handed. The secret of this technique lies in getting my opponent to step backwards in order to create the space I need to make the turn. This is a big movement and the thrower must cover a good deal of distance so the movement has to be fast, bold and committed. The action of the right hand is crucial in 'steering' *uke* to make him step as I want him to, and to ensure that his left hand grip on my sleeve does not prevent me from turning in when I want to.

a) I step forward on my left foot and bend at the waist allowing my arms to almost straighten and hang my weight on *uke* for a second as if I were trying to make him bend at the waist.

b) Then I give a little push with my right hand as I release the pressure to get *uke* moving backwards.

c) As he retreats, withdrawing his left leg I take a big step with my right foot placing it just inside and in front of his right foot. In a smooth, continuous movement I spin on the ball of my right foot, turning my hips through 180 degrees as I place my left foot outside and in front of his left foot.

d) Using both arms to pull myself in to *uke* as soon as my left foot touches the ground my weight transfers onto it and I drive my right leg across in front of *uke*. By bending my knees I get well under his centre of gravity and the momentum generated by my body dropping underneath him should have completely unbalanced him by this point.

e) My legs straighten as I pull him over the outstretched right leg, which helps to flick him over as it straightens. It is important to pull down strongly with both arms to pull him over.

Pulling Tai-Otoshi

a) I withdraw my left leg swinging it behind.

b) As my left foot touches the ground, both hands are pulling upwards and to *uke*'s front, to draw him off-balance over his right foot as my right leg shoots across in front of him to block him from stepping.

c) As he overbalances my bent right leg straightens forcefully causing him to tip forwards.

d) *Uke* trips over my extended right leg.

Sideways Tai-Otoshi

The success of this technique relies on bold, confident movement.

a) I grip *uke* and move sideways as I would to do *okuri-ashi-harai* or *yoko-tomoe-nage*.

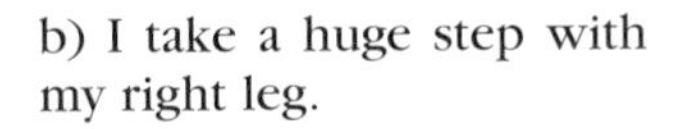

b) I take a huge step with my right leg.

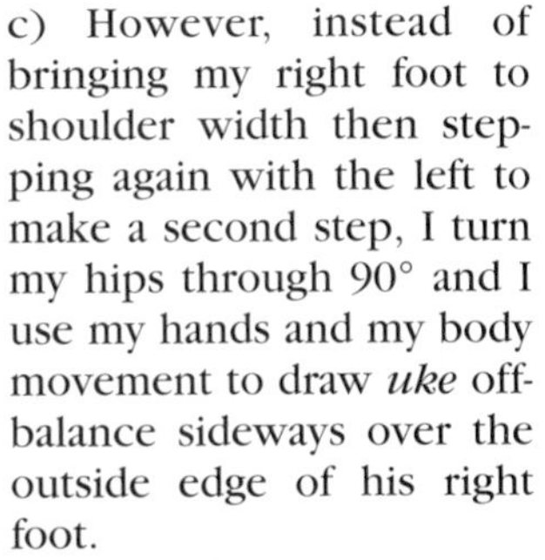

c) However, instead of bringing my right foot to shoulder width then stepping again with the left to make a second step, I turn my hips through 90° and I use my hands and my body movement to draw *uke* off-balance sideways over the outside edge of his right foot.

d) Capitalising on the momentum generated by the step and pull movement I step across and block his right leg with mine and drive him over.

e) *Uke* is flung over!

Tip: make sure to create enough space to step across in front of *uke* and to make sure you bend the knee of the attacking leg so that you can make best use of the extra thrust generated by the straightening action.

Arm Trap Tai-Otoshi

This type of *tai-otoshi* is a bit of an opportunist's technique and is very popular among Eastern European and Russian fighters.

a) As *uke* tries to slip his left arm under my right arm and around my back, I release my grip on his lapel.

b) I slip around and under his left arm and grab hold of his left lapel. This traps his right arm.

Tip: do not wait for *uke* to get a good grip with his left hand. Trap his arm and attack while he is still feeling for his grip.

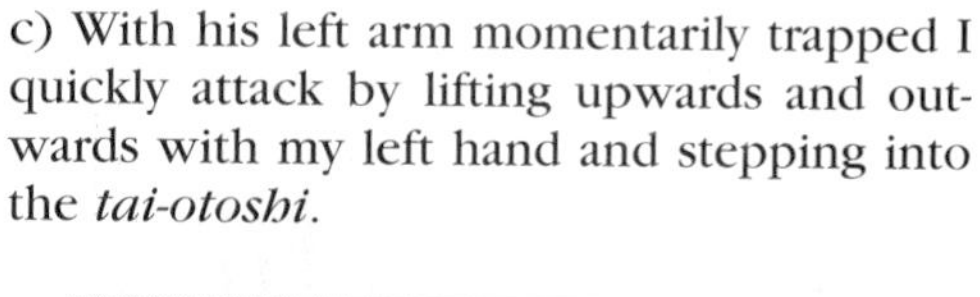

c) With his left arm momentarily trapped I quickly attack by lifting upwards and outwards with my left hand and stepping into the *tai-otoshi*.

d) *Uke* is tripped over my extended right leg.

e) *Ippon* is inevitable.

A closer look at the arm trap from two different perspectives:

Angle I a)

Angle II a)

Angle I b)

Angle II b)

High Collar Tai-Otoshi

Although the high collar grip has certain disadvantages from a defensive viewpoint, especially if your opponent specialises in *seoi-nage,* it is favoured by big, tall men in particular for doing throws like *uchimata* and *harai-goshi*. The great advantage it affords is that of head control.

a) I take a deep collar grip, the thumb inside the jacket, the fingers outside.

b) Stepping forward on my right foot I use my right hand grip to pull *uke*'s head forward and break his balance to his right front as I pull up and out with my left hand.

Tip: Experiment with a high grip that is not quite so deep. Keep the thumb outside the jacket and twist the wrist so that the little finger edge of the hand rests on *uke*'s collar-bone.

c) I spin on my right foot and take my left foot behind, slightly in front and outside of *uke*'s right foot.

d) I stab my right foot in front of *uke* …

e) …and pull him over my outstretched right leg.

Head Lock Tai-Otoshi

This is a variation on the high collar grip and is quite often seen in contest.

a) We are gripping each other with high grips, in an *ai-yotsu* situation.

b) I quickly wrap my right arm around his neck as I come in for the attack.

c) The strong head control allows for a powerful forward pull.

d) *Uke* is whipped off his feet.

e) A definite *ippon*.

Tai-Otoshi as a Counter to High Grip

This is a technique that must be done quickly and suddenly to succeed. It works best when *uke* is just taking a firm hold.

a) I have *uke*'s right sleeve with my left hand and *uke* takes a high grip on my collar with his left hand.

b) I immediately go under his arm with my right hand, so that my biceps comes into contact with his triceps and drive my arm upwards, hooking his arm as I turn, breaking his grip.

Tip: This is an excellent technique to develop on your weaker side and is especially useful against players who like to take a high, dominating grip.

c) I continue my turn, attacking with *tai-otoshi*.

d) The unusual gripping makes for good leverage in pulling him over.

e) *Uke* is rotated over.

Noriko Anno (JPN) attacks with a cross grip *tai-otoshi* which also happens to be my favourite technique.

Cross Grip Tai-Otoshi

This was one of my special techniques for many years and I scored *ippon* on many occasions with it. It is especially useful against very strong, extreme right-handed fighters.

a) I begin by adopting a standard cross grip, right hand on *uke*'s right lapel, fingers inside and grip his right sleeve just below the elbow with my left hand.

b) I make a very quick attack, stepping across with my right leg.

c) The cross grip allows for a very strong pull on *uke*'s right side. Notice that my right leg is slightly bent.

d) I straighten my right leg and *uke* is popped upwards and over.

e) A perfect throw!

My favourite technique: the cross-grip *tai-otoshi.*

a) From my favourite grip, I enter with my right leg bent.

b) I straighten my right leg as I whip him over.

c) I love this throw!

Cross Grip Tai-Otoshi—The Wave

This was one of the special techniques of the Japanese middleweight Shinobu Sekine, a world and Olympic middleweight champion who was a specialist in fighting with one sided grips and who developed his own very special timing and rhythm which made his techniques doubly effective.

a) I take a cross grip with my right hand on his right lapel, standing right side slightly forwards.

b) I take a big step back on my left foot, bending my knees. I also bend at the waist, smoothly pulling *uke* down and forwards so that he doubles over and must take a step to forwards to recover his balance.

c) Next, I step across with my right foot, releasing the pressure on *uke* and begin to straighten up. *Uke*'s natural reaction after having been bent forwards will be to straighten up, following your movement.

d) I quickly pull and slip underneath his arm with a cross grip *tai-otoshi*.

e) *Uke* is drawn over my extended right leg.

f) *Ippon*!

Tip: It is vital to practise this on the move and get the correct timing. Tense your back muscles almost as if you were doing a pull up as you make your back step and bend your opponent, then relax completely allowing him to rise of his own accord. This step and the correct co-ordination of tension and relaxation is the key to the special timing of this throw.

Double Lapel Tai-Otoshi

The big advantage of taking the mid-chest grip with both hands is that *uke*'s shoulders are well controlled, and supple, skilful players can attack right or left as the opportunities present themselves, making it very difficult to predict what they are going to do. The main drawback with this method is that since *uke*'s sleeve is not gripped he may be able to put his arm out to block the throw.

a) Initially I step back, away from *uke* creating the space I need to turn in.

b) I make a sudden big step forward on my right foot and pull with my hands as if I were going to come in with a left-handed *osoto-gari*, provoking *uke* into stiffening defensively and, ideally, leaning his weight forwards.

c) As he reacts, putting most of his weight on his forward right leg I change, throw my left leg around behind me, pull up with both arms and stamp my right foot across in front of his right leg. The back of my bent knee should catch him just under his knee.

d) I continue to pull and turn my shoulders as my leg straightens, making him airborne.

Double-Sleeve Tai-Otoshi

During the era of tailored judo kits and tight fitting jackets this technique was rarely seen. But with the rule changes introduced in the 1990s, and sleeves that can be gripped more easily, the re-emergence of *sode-tsuri-komi-goshi* and all its variants as effective *ippon* scoring techniques has been dramatic.

a) It all starts off with a non-gripping situation.

b) As we come to grips, I reach for the ends of both his sleeves.

c) Without hesitation I turn in with a *sode-tsuri-komi-goshi* movement.

d) However, instead of loading him onto my back I just pull him forward, and trip him over my extended right leg.

Tip: Against a taller opponent the hand action should feel very similar to a normal *tai-otoshi*. Against someone shorter though, it can be easier and more effective to drive the right arm up in the air and make more contact with the hip.

Single-Sleeve Tai-Otoshi I

This technique is a speciality of Michael Swain of the USA, the 1987 world champion. One problem with right *tai-otoshi* is what to do when faced with a determined opponent who will not let you grip his left lapel or who strongly controls your right sleeve, which is a standard defence or way of neutralising the danger. This is an ingenious solution to the problem.

a) I have my right hand grip on *uke*'s left sleeve, but he is controlling my right sleeve, stopping me from gripping his left lapel with my right hand.

b) I quickly slip my hand across and drive my open palm into his right forearm just below the crook of his elbow.

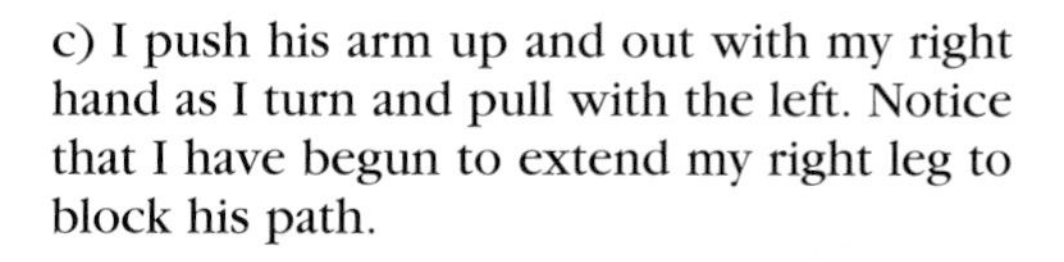

c) I push his arm up and out with my right hand as I turn and pull with the left. Notice that I have begun to extend my right leg to block his path.

d) My bent right leg now completely blocks his right leg.

e) As I pull him off balance my leg straightens forcefully, flicking him over as my hands drive him to the floor.

Tip: This technique is especially effective precisely because *uke* thinks he has strong control of my right sleeve and there is no danger of me being able to turn in with *tai-otoshi*. However even though *uke* may control my sleeve, he does not control my hand and it is usually an easy matter to reach his right forearm or wrist with my right hand. As I turn, his blocking (left) arm is completely nullified.

Single-Sleeve Tai-Otoshi II

Against an opponent who likes to hold with a very strong right hand grip on your left lapel a useful ploy is to use two hands to break his grip and attack immediately before he re-grips.

a) My opponent has a very strong right hand grip.

b) I reach over with my right hand and grab his wrist with both of my hands.

c) I break off his grip…

d) …and immediately turn in for *tai-otoshi*.

Wrong Leg Tai-Otoshi

The origins of this technique are uncertain but anyone who has specialised in *tai-otoshi* sooner or later encounters the situation where the person being attacked manages to step over the attacking leg yet is still thrown because of the hand action. The logical conclusion, then, is that the throw can be done against either leg! In the early and mid-seventies the British light heavyweight Dave Starbrook used this technique to very good effect in international competition.

a) My opponent is holding left with his left leg forward and I am holding right and standing sideways on with my right leg forward.

b) I step in, in normal *tai-otoshi* fashion, throwing my left leg around behind me and pulling up with both hands.

c) However, instead of stepping across with my right leg I drive it back between *uke*'s legs. as my foot touches the ground I straighten the leg forcefully, knocking *uke*'s left leg up in the air and driving his weight over his right foot.

d) The pull with the hands is now completely downwards, trapping uke on his advanced right foot. Because his weight is pinned on his foot he cannot step to adjust his posture and he is pulled completely off balance over his foot and thrown.

a) David Starbrook (Britain) feared for his awesome strength, attacks Jan Bosman of the Netherlands with his brand of *tai-otoshi*.

b) The Dutchman manages to step over Starbrook's blocking leg.

c) Nevertheless, he is rotated over by Starbrook. A classic "wrong leg" *tai-otoshi!*

Wide-Split Tai-Otoshi

Sometimes against short or crouching opponents who keep their centre of gravity very low it can be desirable to come in really low. Some fighters like to drop on one knee to achieve this, but I have never liked that kind of entry. A better alternative is to go for a wider split—if you are supple enough. Phil Takahashi of Canada and my team-mate, Densign White, used to do this kind of deep, low *tai-otoshi* and got some good results with it.

a) Both *uke* and I are holding right handed.

b) I take a big step forward on my right foot, stepping just in front and inside of *uke*'s left foot, and almost simultaneously, make a big, wide step around behind me with my left foot.

c) Then, placing it about a foot wide of *uke*'s left foot and slightly in front of it, I complete the move by shooting my right leg across into this blocking position.

d) I make a long pull up with my left hand. I reach as far across in front of *uke* as I can with my right foot without overstretching and collapsing. The ideal contact is still the back of my bent knee with *uke*'s leg just below the knee, but because my left foot is much wider than normal I have to reach further and get lower to attain it.

e) As my weight drops under *uke* into a fully stretched position he is pulled off balance forwards.

f) The leg straightening as the hands pull down generates a lot of power and the fall, though not especially high, is a hard, fast one.

a) My compatriot Densign White and his wide-split *tai-otoshi*.

b) My wide split *tai-otoshi*.

Jumping (Spinning) Tai-Otoshi

This is a dynamic *tai-otoshi*, utilising the momentum of your entry to hurl *uke* over. Interestingly enough, this happens to be the *tokui-waza* of Ippon Books's photographer: David Finch!

a) My opponent and I are facing each other squarely. I am pushing into him slightly, to get him to push back.

b) I make a diagonal step with my left foot, tugging *uke*'s right elbow as I do so, making him feel there is a danger of a left-side rear attack.

c) As he stiffens and pushes forward to kill my movement, I make a quick spin in the air.

d) I land with my right leg fully extended. The momentum of the spin causes him to pitch forward.

e) The throw is a heavy one!

Tai-Otoshi as a Counter I Against Osoto-Gari

This sort of technique is often produced spontaneously by children in *randori* and early gradings, without them having been taught it as a formal counter to *osoto-gari*.

a) My opponent comes in with *osoto-gari*. I anticipate his attack and rather than waiting to give him contact I immediately counter attack. At this stage it looks like it is going to be *osoto-gaeshi* but I have something else in mind.

b) Instead of attacking his attacking leg, I attack his supporting leg with *tai-otoshi*. He is taken by surprise and is put off balance by my unusual response.

c) The *osoto-gari* is successfully countered!

Tai-Otoshi as a Counter II
Uchimata-Sukashi

In some cases people throw themselves completely without *tori* doing very much at all, other than managing to avoid the initial attack.

a) My opponent attacks with *uchimata*, but I have anticipated this and put most of my weight on my left foot as his leg comes in.

b) I lift my right foot and sidestep his attack.

c) As his leg swings through and his body bends forwards I shoot my right leg across in front of him and use my hands to throw him with *tai-otoshi*.

d) The faster and more committed the *uchimata* attack the better.

In my first fight at the 1984 Los Angeles Olympics, I faced the canny Robert Henneveld (NED). After a fierce exchange of grips, I attacked him with a very low *tai-otoshi*. The Dutchman tried to block the attack but ended up loaded completely onto my back. I straightened my legs and threw him over with *seoi-otoshi*. It was an unintentional combination but it worked brilliantly!

COMBINATIONS

One of the beauties of developing a good, fast *tai-otoshi* is that the process inevitably involves an increase in movement skills and agility, which are transferable factors when it comes to doing other techniques. *Tai-otoshi* is generally a large, open movement which means that it lends itself well to combinations with other throws. Combinations are of two types, *renraku-waza*, where one throw flows into another one in the same direction and *renzoku-waza* where there is a sudden decisive change of direction, exploiting an opponent's strong defensive reaction to throw him.

Techniques into Tai-Otoshi
Ouchi-Gari -> Tai-Otoshi

Ouchi-gari is the perfect technique to develop in combination with many forward throws especially *tai-otoshi*, because it is in the opposite direction and a strong defensive reaction to either technique paves the way for using the other one. In addition *tai-otoshi* is very good against people who like to keep their feet fairly close together, while *ouchi-gari* is effective against wide stances. The key to making them complement one another is to make the entry for both as similar as possible until the last possible second.

Ouchi-gari—>Tai-otoshi I (Follow-Up)

This combination involves making a committed attack with *ouchi-gari* and forcing *uke to* defend by stepping off the attack. This creates the space necessary and alters his stance to make an effective attack with *tai-otoshi*.

a) *Uke* has a left grip with his left leg forward—a disadvantageous position for me to attack with a direct *tai-otoshi*.

b) I attack with an *ouchi-gari* to open him up and to get him to push forward.

c) He lifts his left leg to avoid the throw. He is wary of the attack and will push forward to avoid frustrate my attack.

d) As soon as his left foot touches the ground I begin making my entry for the follow-up attack, making full use of his resistance and forward push.

e) My push to the rear turns into a pull to his front as I launch myself into a *tai-otoshi* against his forward leg, which is the right one at this point.

f) He is tripped over my extended right leg.

g) A perfect combination!

Ouchi-gari—>Tai-Otoshi II (Double-Motion)

This is a classic combination that is particularly popular in Japan.

a) I face *uke* in a *kenka-yotsu* situation.

b) I launch into an *ouchi-gari* attack.

c) This elicits the reaction that I want. Notice that *uke* is already pushing forwards to avoid being thrown backwards.

d) I immediately switch into a very fast and very low *tai-otoshi*.

e) *Uke* goes flying over!

Kosoto-Gari—>Tai-Otoshi

Often favoured by taller, long-legged men this technique can be adapted to suit players of different heights. The direction of the *tai-otoshi* that follows the initial *kosoto-gari* attack is determined by how big a step *uke* makes to save himself. This is in turn often determined by the amount of energy in the initial *kosoto-gari*.

a) In order to attack effectively with *tai-otoshi* I need to make *uke* move his left leg, which is blocking my entry.

b) Pulling down and bending my knees so that my bodyweight is brought to bear on *uke*, I step forward and place my right foot just behind his left heel.

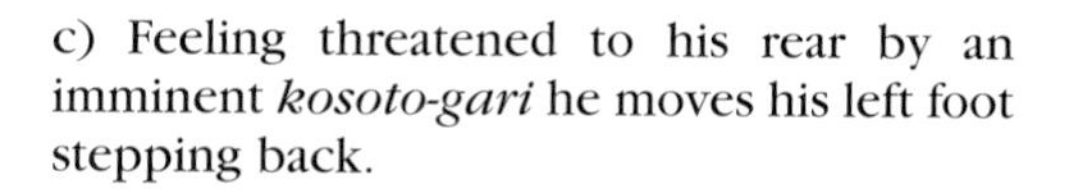

c) Feeling threatened to his rear by an imminent *kosoto-gari* he moves his left foot stepping back.

d) Now even though he is holding left, his posture is right and the gate is open for me to step in with my *tai-otoshi* and throw him forwards.

e) I quickly turn in with the familiar *tai-otoshi* movement…

f) ...extend my right leg...

Tip: Do not try to actually sweep his leg when you step in to do *kosoto-gari*, just place your foot there to get him to move his. Bear down on him with your hands when you step in and when you feel he wants to move just relax and let him. It is not necessary to push him to his rear—in fact pushing him would give the game away.

g) ...and throw him over!

Kouchi-Gari—>Tai-Otoshi

Kouchi-gari is a good technique for opening up defensive opponents and is usually fairly safe.

a) *Uke* is right handed and has a strong right arm grip and right leg forward. His right leg is too far forward for me to attack comfortably with *tai-otoshi*, so I use *kouchi-gari* to manoeuvre him into a better throwing position.

b) I use my right foot to clip *uke*'s right foot just at his heel and pull down with both hands.

c) *Uke* steps back to avoid being knocked down by the *kouchi-gari* attack and now his posture is more square on and I can attack with *tai-otoshi*.

d) I immediately pivot on my right leg to turn into *tai-otoshi*.

e) I step across with my right leg, as usual.

f) *Uke* goes over.

Techniques from Tai-Otoshi

Tai-Otoshi—>Tomoe-Nage

This was a technique I only began to use later in my career, but it worked extremely well on a number of occasions.

a) I attack with a cross-grip right *tai-otoshi* and *uke* stiffens to block my effort.

b) As *uke* is obviously not going over, I come out of the attack.

c) And immediately go into *yoko-tomoe-nage*.

d) *Uke* is thrown towards my right side.

e) I use both my arms to guide his fall, to ensure that he lands on his back.

Tip: The *tai-otoshi* attack must be a real attempt to throw him in order to get him to react and stiffen defensively. Also he has to feel you are there one moment and gone the next. He will relax feeling, that the danger has passed—and that is when you must switch straight into *tomoe-nage*.

Tai-Otoshi—>Uchimata

I will never forget throwing Takahiro Nishida of Japan, whom I always considered to be one of my most dangerous opponents, for a spectacular *ippon* with this combination in the 1978 Kano Cup.

a) I attack with *tai-otoshi*.

b) However, *uke* has managed to step over my extended right leg.

c) He feels relatively safe now, having escaped the first attack.

d) Before he composes himself, I step straight into *uchimata*.

e) *Uke* flies!

Tai-Otoshi—>Ippon-Seoi-Nage

This is a 180 degree change of direction that many defenders find difficult to cope with.

a) I attack *uke* with a strong, fast right *tai-otoshi*, forcing him to move to avoid being thrown.

b) He escapes the first attack.

c) Having steered clear of the attack, we are almost facing each other squarely.

d) Before he can compose himself, though, I spin in for *ippon-seoi-nage* (to the other side).

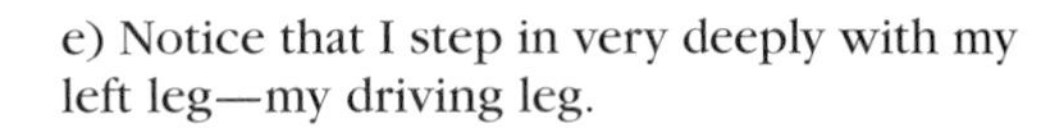

e) Notice that I step in very deeply with my left leg—my driving leg.

f) *Uke* goes flying over…

Tai-Otoshi—>Juji-Gatame

One of my favourite *tachiwaza* into *newaza* combinations was always *tai-otoshi* into *juji-gatame*. I honed it to contest sharpness by doing thousands of repetitions. It is difficult to do at high level because when top competitors get thrown they usually twist onto their faces immediately to avoid the danger of getting caught in this way. But occasionally it can come off. I scored *waza-ari* on Jacobson of Denmark in the 1981 European Championships in Debrecen, with *tai-otoshi* and followed it up instantly with *juji-gatame* to score *ippon*.

a) I throw *uke* with a *tai-otoshi*.

b) As he has only landed on his side, I must finish him off with a newaza follow-up.

c) I immediately sit down into *juji-gatame* position.

d) Submission is quick.

DEFENCES AND COUNTERS

One of the main reasons that *tai-otoshi* has always been a popular technique among those judo players with a positive, attacking philosophy is that it is not an easy throw to counter. *Tai-otoshi* specialists can attack again and again with the same movement and if they are strong attacks the best that the opponent can usually hope for is to avoid or block.

The general principles usually involved in judo teaching follow a logical progression. Players learn a technique, then they learn an avoidance or blocking movement and then a counter. Blocking is generally only considered in a very cursory way, mainly because the most difficult thing to achieve in judo teaching terms is to get people to develop positive attacking movements.

A good all round defence usually consists of four elements, posture, balance, stability and responsiveness. In contest, some players concentrate on standing up straight, gripping hard and using the strength of their arms to keep their opponents at bay. Others go into a deep crouch and break grip at the slightest hint of a technique, others move around freely and easily relying on anticipation and movement skills to keep them out of trouble. At some point or other in virtually everyone's judo career it becomes necessary to defend in each of these ways.

Different opponents elicit different responses. In *randori* the best defence has to be based on freedom of movement and adaptability, mainly because it encourages good attacking movement among both partners.

Almost everyone's natural tendency in *randori* is to avoid the danger of being thrown. They do this in different ways. Some are reluctant to move and plant themselves firmly, trying to use strong arms and awkward grips. Others move around a lot, but continually break off their partners' grips without mounting any real attacks themselves. There is even a kind of player who is aggressive in a passive way, making numerous incorrect attacking movements with little or no hope of throwing his partner purely to forestall being thrown himself. These are all bad, negative ways to practise.

The element of sport, fun and excitement that is so high in judo comes from risk-taking. Sometimes to bring off spectacular techniques you have to take a risk and commit yourself. If you get countered you get countered, that is the essence of the game. This all or nothing spirit is what characterises the judo of the great champions. Of course it is not always so easy to practise in this way if your partners do not want to cooperate. Many people pick up bad habits over the years and sometimes rather than just scrapping away with a negative, defensive training partner it is worth getting into a dialogue and discussing or explaining just what you are trying to achieve from the practice.

While awkward, hard to throw, defensive partners may be just what a championship competitor needs once his techniques are polished, just to hone that final edge needed to be contest effective and confirm his confidence in his techniques, for the player trying to develop new skills it is a different story. A certain amount of give and take is vital. It is a good idea to remind people of Dr. Kano's fundamental maxims from time to time. Even the most stubborn defenders can be persuaded to get into the spirit of give and take and mutual benefit if the idea is explained to them in the right way. Communication is extremely important among all the members of a club and it is the instructor or sensei's job to make sure that everyone knows why they are practising and how to practise in such a way as to achieve maximum benefits.Skill training does not have to be boring and while everyone likes a good tussle in *randori*, it is a lot more satisfying if it is a skilful tussle!

The normal learning sequence is to study how to avoid and block *tai-otoshi* then the next stage is to practise developing counters to the technique. There are two basic approaches to blocking the technique. The first involves controlling the grips so that a *tai-otoshi* attack is impossible. This is normally achieved either by controlling the attacker's right sleeve and preventing him from turning in, or by tearing the arm free and blocking with the hips as he attacks, or in the case of a weak or off-balance attack by using your bodyweight to squash the technique. The standard avoidance is to step over the attacking leg and turn so as to face the attacker.

One of the reasons that *tai-otoshi* is so difficult to counter is that people generally do not train in specialised counter techniques unless they come across a particular rival who happens to have a strong *tai-otoshi*. Effective counter techniques do exist however. Although some are more risky than others, they can all be made to work, especially in the case of a careless or weak *tai-otoshi*.

Breaking Away

This is the simple basic blocking action commonly used against most forward attacks, here slightly modified to frustrate a *tai-otoshi* attack.

a) My opponent attacks with *tai-otoshi*.

b) As I feel him come in I twist my hips and pull back my right shoulder.

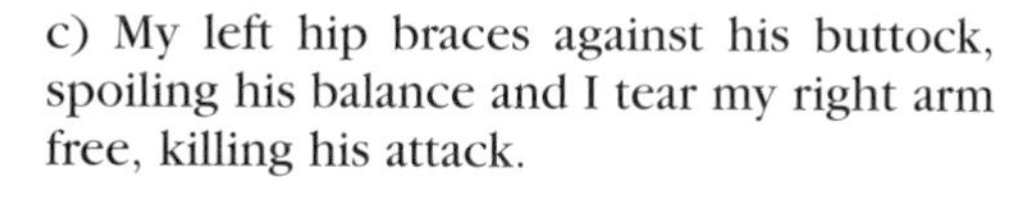

c) My left hip braces against his buttock, spoiling his balance and I tear my right arm free, killing his attack.

I break away in order to foil my opponent's attempt at *tai-otoshi*.

Yoko-Guruma

This counter technique is popular among heavyweights and makes use of the energy in my opponent's attack to throw him. Being a sacrifice technique there is a certain amount of risk involved, not least because the referee may interpret the attempt to counter as a too-late response to being thrown. Although an uninterrupted movement is desirable, it is important to make it clear that you have avoided or controlled the attack when you do this technique.

a) My opponent comes in for a *tai-otoshi* attack.

b) I stop his attack by wrapping my left arm round his waist and stepping around him.

c) I make a complete rotation, arching my back as I do so.

d) I actually sacrifice to the ground. My right hand pushes as the left pulls and I rotate to my left, looking over my shoulder as I throw him. Notice that I have extended my left leg to block his right leg.

e) As I fall to the ground, I turn on my left side and rotate him over.

f) The momentum of my rotation and sacrificing movement causes him to land flat on his back.

Tip: Be ready to follow up immediately with *newaza* and practise securing *yoko-shiho-gatame* from this throw.

Kosoto-Gake

This is the classic counter to *tai-otoshi*.

a) My opponent comes in for a *tai-otoshi* attack.

b) I step around his right leg to avoid the technique.

c) I counter-attack with a left-sided *kosoto-gake*.

d) I hook in deeply and put all my weight to take him backwards.

e) The hooking action of my left leg and the weight of my body causes his feet to come off the ground.

f) *Ippon*...a perfect counter.

Tip: against a determined attack it is important to step and rotate at the same time, so that you have turned to face your attacker as your right foot touches the floor.

a) I attack my opponent, Ramon Pink (GDR) with *tai-otoshi*.

b) To my great surprise, he manages to counter me with *kosoto-gake*! Fortunately I went on to win the contest.

Tani-Otoshi

The key point in using *tani-otoshi* as a counter is the direction of the throw. Many people try to do it by resisting their partner's attack and pulling him in the direct opposite direction. This is hard work and not usually very effective. The trick is to block the initial attack then push to your left side and slightly forwards if he is pulling that way. If the direction is correct he will lose his balance easily and completely. Only once he is weightless and actually falling do you direct his fall backwards by twisting your body and pulling with your arms, so that he lands on his back, not his hip and shoulder. This is quite a subtle point, but makes all the difference.

a) My opponent has attacked me with a determined *tai-otoshi*. I block by bending my knees, making sure to get my hips below his and catch his hip bone with my left hand.

b) I sit down, pushing him to his side and slightly forwards, blocking his left foot with the side of my left leg.

c) As he begins to fall sideways and forwards I rotate my upper body and pull him backwards over my blocking leg.

Koshi-Jime

As *tai-otoshi*, like drop *seoi-nage*, is a fairly safe throw to attack with, it lends itself to repeated attacks. It is possible to lose a contest if the other player attacks more. It may not be possible to counter a particular opponent's *tai-otoshi* with a throw every time, particularly if he is using the technique tactically. One answer is to smother the attack and counter attack with groundwork.

a) My opponent comes in with *tai-otoshi* and I block by opening my legs, dropping my hips and sinking my centre of gravity.

b) My left hand catches his left hip or I slip it inside his thigh to assist with controlling him and my right hand pulls him to the floor.

c) I can now strangle him by pulling his lapel tight against his neck and using my right wrist to do *koshi-jime*.

d) I use my hips to exert the additional pressure necessary to make the strangle work.

Since a teenager, World and Olympic champion, Yasuhiro Yamashita worked to develop *tai-otoshi* as a back-up to his other major throws: *uchimata, ouchi-gari* and *osoto-gar*i. Despite years of training, he couldn't get it to work. In the semi-final of his very last competition, the 1995 All-Japan Championships, Yamashita was making heavy weather against the rising star of Japanese judo, Yoshimi Masaki, when out of the blue he produced a very low *tai-otoshi.* It scored *yuko* and allowed him to finish off the young upstart on the ground. Yamashita later said "In the end I was saved by the technique which I couldn't get right since I started learning it it in the second year of high school."

Training For Tai-Otoshi

The basis of training for *tai-otoshi* is the same as for any other throwing technique: *uchikomi*, *nage-komi* and *randori*. These three methods have proven their worth time and again and perhaps the most important consideration is that of getting the balance between the three right.

There are many things to pay attention to in the course of perfecting a *tai-otoshi*: grip, stance, foot movements, pulling actions of each hand, head position, hip turn, knee bend, points of contact, depth of entry and last but not least, the opponent. Differences in height, weight and reach generally require some kind of adaptation for a throw to be successful. Top competitors often train with particular rivals in mind and look for training partners who present the same sort of problem in terms of grip, stature and even strategy.

Uchikomi

Traditionally beginners do a lot of *uchikomi*, to get the steps right and learn to co-ordinate head, hands and feet so that they do not overbalance and fall over as they try to do the throw. Normally, to simplify the situation they are taught to do *tai-otoshi* against a static *uke*, but it is important to progress methodically to doing it in different movement situations against partners who step forwards, backward, sideways and soon.

Static *uchikomi* on its own is too restricted and if the opponent is moving he will be easier to throw than if he is stationary, which is an important consideration that beginners should grasp right from the start.

Tai-otoshi is quite a complex movement so there is a lot to pay attention to in order to get it right. I am a firm believer in teaching *uchikomi* as an integral part of the throwing movement, not as something separate from the throw: each set of *uchikomi* should end with a completion. One of the problems of doing only *uchikomi* is that the trainee learns to stop the throw, sometimes before learning to complete it. While this is good from the point of view of discipline and control, and in a practical sense necessary in order to develop the movement, it can develop into a fault if not balanced out with regular *nage-komi*.

Uchikomi ought not to be slapdash or mindless. Many players do their *uchikomi* as if they were doing press-ups, as a kind of unthinking warm up. There is nothing wrong with doing *uchikomi* to warm up, but it should never be unthinking; the aim of the exercise is to develop skill. This is best achieved by concentrating on specific points while gradually developing the general movement. The ideal is to make each repetition the same and mechanically perfect. Sets of 10, throwing on the 10th repetition is the most widespread form of practising 'static' *uchikomi*. The limited size of most dojos tends to mean moving *uchikomi* gets done in sets of three to five, the important thing is that the movements should be complete and alive.

As *tai-otoshi* is a hand throw it is vital to get both hands working correctly. Many beginners find they lose their grip with one hand or the other, usually because they are not gripping correctly. An excellent drill to correct these problems is one-handed *uchikomi*.

Tsurite Uchikomi

This is the name given to *uchikomi* done with only the lapel grip—the right hand in a right handed *tai-otoshi*. *Tori* can put his left hand in his belt and practise turning in, concentrating on the drawing action of the right hand. Practise holding with a straight, relaxed thumb as this makes it easier to relax the forearm and shoulder, which are quite often tense and make it difficult for people to relax and turn in. The action varies from individual to individual and the type of *tai-otoshi* they do, but generally has feeling of being a smooth pull, that turns into a push. Once a good level of skill has been developed it is possible to practise throwing *uke*, using only the right hand. *Uke* must be experienced and keep hold with his right hand when he gets thrown so as to be able to fall correctly.

a) I turn in for the one-handed attack with only a grip on *uke*'s left lapel.

b) My right leg is now fully extended. Notice that I've got my *hikite* arm (right hand) tucked into my belt.

c) Although I do not have a grip with my left hand, I am able to turn *uke* over by taking full advantage of his strong grip on my left collar.

e) *Uke* is thrown over.

Note: Although this exercise is aimed at developing proper leg movements, this variation can actually work in competition. World champion, Michael Swain of the USA used this variation successfully against various top international competitors. Of course, he didn't have his *hikite* arm tucked in his belt when he attacked!

Hikite Uchikomi

This is *uchikomi* designed to perfect the action of the *hikite* or sleeve grip.

a) I pull upwards and outwards with my hikite hand (sleeve grip). I turn my hand so that I can see the back of my wrist, the little finger edge of the hand turned up towards the ceiling. (This action is often described as an exaggerated form of looking at your watch to tell the time). Notice that this time I have tucked my right hand in my belt.

b) Next, I drop down low and extend my right leg.

c) I pull hard with my *hikite* grip as I straighten my right leg.

d) *Uke* is pulled over.

Nage-Komi

The same comments as have been made about *uchikomi* apply equally well to *nage-komi*, but there are some important differences. The basic requirement to do effective *nage-komi* is a sprung floor. This is not a luxury, but a basic need which all judo clubs should aim to have sooner rather than later. Without a sprung floor *nage-komi* tends not to be a very popular activity. For the club player, if there is no sprung floor, practise throwing, but without finishing so decisively, so as to make your partners' falls easier to take. *Nage-komi* is best practised in groups of five or six, each person throwing the other people in the group five times. Most people can handle being thrown five times in succession with the same technique, but anymore than five can be a bit too much.

As with *uchikomi* aim for the perfect throw each time. Do not sacrifice form for speed. Often people rush to get the throws done and the effectiveness of the training is reduced. Take your time and make each entry a decisive ippon scoring technique. Do the throw fast by all means, but make sure you get the movement and timing right, do not be rushed into doing it wrong! *Tai-otoshi* is a very precise movement requiring a lot of co-ordination and it helps if you have an intelligent *uke* who can cooperate with you in terms of gripping and moving as you need him to to practise properly.

Five sets of five throws may not sound like a lot, but if you train four times a week it is a hundred complete throws. Ask yourself how long it takes you to score a hundred ippons in *randori*. Unless you are exceptionally good the answer is likely to be a lot longer than a week!

Randori

Randori is of course one of the most important training methods within judo, but I feel that the best kind of *randori* for developing skill is with about 60% resistance. Thus is particularly true if you repeatedly train with the same partners. Full resistance all the time can be counter productive, and where too much ego is at stake *randori* can degenerate into a mauling session. To encourage creativity and skill progression there has to be a balance, what could be termed "realistic cooperation". The element of play, of give and take is very important in *randori* although sometimes it has to be tailored to specific individuals and situations. There are players who lose interest if they think it is too easy, who thrive psychologically on the challenge of 100 per cent resistance. The beauty of *randori* is its sheer flexibility and the training stimulus for such players can easily be modified.

There are all sorts of variations that can be introduced into randori from time to time when trying to develop a particular technique. One player can be limited to attacking with one or two techniques, the other to only avoiding or blocking or holding with one hand; or being limited to only being allowed to try a particular counter. The permutations are many and can be very useful for solving specific problems that different players may have.

Rubber Bands

Apart from these traditional methods there are other drills that can be especially useful in developing *tai-otoshi*. I found rubber bands to be helpful for developing fast footwork and the co-ordination between the hands and feet. They can provide variety and allow you to do hundreds of repetitions without complaint if you loop them around wall bars or a pillar or column of some kind. A padded pillar such as the one Dave Starbrook used to train against at the Renshuden is ideal because you can also practise and strengthen the leg contact. There are various, excellent rubber training aids available commercially, but old bicycle or moped inner tubes can be just as useful if you cannot afford them and do not mind getting your hands dirty.

Nikolai Ojeguine (RUS) attacks former world champion, Ryuji Sonoda (JPN), with a very low, drop *tai-otoshi* in the final of the -60 kg division. Although the attack did not score, it was techniques like this that allowed him to win the gold medal. 1995 Tokyo World Championships.

Competition Tai-Otoshi

Tai-otoshi has been used decisively by a number of champions at top level competition. One of the most famous *tai-otoshi* men of all time was Isao Inokuma. Standing just 1m 73 and never weighing much over 83 kg, Isao Inokuma was a very small man to be competing in the heavy and open weight categories at world and Olympic judo tournaments, but he made up for his lack of inches and pounds with a devastating combination of skill,power and fighting spirit. He began life as a *seoi-nage* specialist, particularly *ippon-seoi-nage* but after losing in the semi-finals of the 1959 All-Japan Judo tournament to Akio Kaminaga he realised that having just one major technique made him too predictable and somewhat limited. As a result he added *tai-otoshi* to his repertoire and had some spectacular success with it, becoming All-Japan, World and Olympic Champion. He used to combine right *tai-otoshi* with right *ippon-seoinage* in a way that made it very difficult to predict which technique he was actually going to use until the last possible moment. He would attack first with one then the other, varying the order, but always looking for the *ippon*.

Isao Inokuma throws Muto with *tai-otoshi* in the 1960 All-Japan Championships.

Interestingly enough, *tai-otoshi* has been in decline in Japan. Of the current Japanese champions few regard *tai-otoshi* as their *tokui-waza*. However, several westerners have brought *tai-otoshi* back into vogue. Among the most notable is Udo Quellmalz, the German double-world champion with remarkable pulling strength.

a) Quellmalz has his opponent totally off balance.

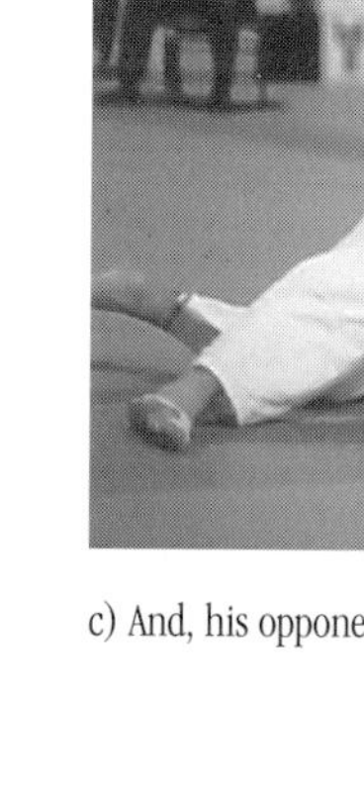

c) And, his opponent is flat on his back

b) A strong rotation.

d) *Ippon!*

1993 Hamilton World Championships

Here we see Quellmalz demolishing his opponent Shturbabin (UZB) in the final of the -71 kg division. Although his opponent manages to step over Quellmalz's blocking leg, the German was able to rotate him over for *ippon*. The hand action is so important in tai-otoshi. 1996 Shoriki Cup in Japan.

There is no question that the score that Quellmalz received from this throw was *ippon*. 1995 Tokyo World Championships.

One of Europe's greatest contribution to judo is the low *tai-otoshi*, an incredibly effective technique. This type of technique is seldom seen in Japan where the classical version is more popular. But in Europe, it is very common.

a) Karen Briggs, one of the originators of the low *tai-otoshi,* attacks with her specialty.

b) From this position it is easy for Briggs to rotate her opponent over.

c) In fact, she over-rotates her partner and has to continue with groundwork!

a) Here Karen Briggs shows her versatility by attacking with a regular *tai-otoshi.*

b) Lynn Poirier of Canada is rotated over Briggs's extended right leg. Note Briggs' particular variation - the turned right foot.

c) *A* perfect throw!

a) French Olympic champion, Marc Alexandre attacks with technique remarkably similar to Karen Briggs's drop *tai-otoshi*.

b) As before, the rotation is relatively easy.

c) Alexandre can now switch to *newaza* to finish off his opponent.

a) World Champion, Sergei Kosorotv of Russia, attacks with an extremely low *tai-otoshi*. It doesn't look like it will work.

b) But it does. Ippon scored!

a) I've also been known to do low *tai-otoshis* now and again!

b) However, notice that my knees are not actually touching the mat.

a) Double Olympic champion, Peter Seisenbacher of Austria, attacks double world champion, Fabien Canu of France, with a wrong leg *tai-otoshi*. 1988 Seoul Olympics

b) Although he only managed to trip Canu's near leg, the effect of the technique is evident. The strong pulling action of the hands is crucial to the success of this technique. 1988 Seoul Olympics

a) Olympic champion Hidehiko Yoshida (JPN) bends his blocking leg while extending his supporting leg—the total opposite of how *tai-otoshi* is normally done.

b) A highly unusual but remarkably effective variation of *tai-otoshi.* 1995 Tokyo World Championships.

EPILOGUE

The last contest I won in my long competition career was in the 1988 Seoul Olympics. I was up against the Portuguese fighter, Pedro Cristovao. After a fierce exchange of grips, and well into the contest, I was able to score *ippon* with a picture-perfect *tai-otoshi*, almost like the full stop at the end of a book.

My favourite throw turned out to be the very last throw of my career. It is a pity that it was not the final...but that is judo.

INDEX

JUDO MASTERCLASS TECHNIQUES SERIES

The most powerful project yet from Ippon Books. For the first time on video, over 60 variations of *tachi-waza,* as used by the greatest and latest stars of judo, are revealed in full detail in this 53-minute broadcast quality production.

For more details about this video title and more, contact:
Ippon Books Ltd, 1st Floor, H.R. House, 447 High Road, North Finchley, London N12 0AF, England. Tel/fax: +44 181-3438210.